Cascade of Stars

BY THE SAME AUTHOR

Yoga: The Iyengar Way
(with Silva and Shyam Mehta)

Health through Yoga

Cascade of Stars

MIRA MEHTA

SHEPHEARD-WALWYN (PUBLISHERS) LTD

First published in 2002 by
Shepheard-Walwyn (Publishers) Ltd
Suite 604, The Chandlery
50 Westminster Bridge Road
London SE1 7QY

British Library Cataloguing in Publication Data
A catalogue record of this book
is available from the British Library

ISBN 0 85683 198 0

Typeset by Alacrity
Banwell Castle, Weston-super-Mare
Printed by St Edmundsbury Press, Bury St Edmunds

❧ To My Dear Mentor

WHO by his words
"You are a poet and an artist born"
And by his acts of understanding
Unstopped the spring of creativity
Which now flows from me
           strong
                and clear
                      and sweet.

AND To My Grandmother

WHO LOOKED UP at the sky
And saw a tornado
Ominously whirling,
In its path all her race.
First sending to safety
Her near ones and dear ones,
She herself braved the night
And the whip of the storm
To gain the same shelter.

CONTENTS

CONTENTS

CONTENTS

CONTENTS

EVERY TIME and clime
Tells anew the tale
Of Cinderella ...

Grieving and distressed
By her mother's death,
Confined to the house
By her day's labours,
Cinderella sings
To console herself.

She explores the world
By way of her mind
And makes a voyage
Questing fate, fortune,
Answers, emotions
And contemplation.

Visited one day
By her godmother,
She is transported
To the fairy realm
Where she is shown signs
That dreams can come true.

Cinderella's world
Extends and expands:
She travels through time
And all creation
With its three pulses,
Life, growth and freedom.

At her journey's end,
Waiting to greet her,
Is a charming Prince ...

CALLING

Cuckoo Clockwork, Cuckoo Imaged

To time's appointment
The miniature bird
In a cuckoo clock
With whirr and flurry
Bursts open the doors
And bursts into song;
Then retires to hibernate
Until its next call.

Like the cuckoo's voice
Mine has riven its gates;
But I shall not return
To latent silence:
My songs will skyward soar
And my words will sound
Through the clear air of Spring,
Bidding wombed Winter
Forever farewell.

DESTINIES
AND DECISIONS

❧ OH, MOTHER!

WHAT DARK THREADS did you choose, my Mother,
To weave on the loom of your life,
For you loved gold and silver, my Mother,
And I remember your singing and laughter.
I remember your courage, my Mother,
For you were always in pain;
And I remember your fear.

You never swerved from the straight, my Mother,
Though you struggled on a stony road.
What was the cost of your choices, my Mother?
You kept silent and never complained.
No stranger to hardship and sorrow, my Mother,
You were forbearing, gentle,
Gifted and witty and strong.

You were loved by your students, my Mother,
For you taught with brilliance and care;
You had deep understanding, my Mother,
High ideals and unselfish ways.
People trusted you with their problems, my Mother,
Knew you would hear them and give
Advice or comfort or aid.

You held fast to your faith, my Mother,
Through a life that tested your all;
You left this gift with your tapestry, my Mother,
Which of all things you valued the most.
Against the dark now the gold glisters, my Mother,
And the silver is sparkling;
May you now rest in peace.

𝒳 Spears and Shields

If you have love to give
And give it,
Once lifelong, as your breath,
And once to one in need,
And it is despised;
If you have beliefs
And live them,
And they prove false
Not once, but twice;
If you have vows to pledge
And they are first unwanted,
Then unneeded;
If you have a mind
That shies from compromise;
How do you survive?

I steeled my heart against bitterness
With piercing pins;
I packed my beliefs in a case
And sent it away;
I exchanged my vows
With freedom;
I set my mind
The task of understanding.

Shake me, break me,
Take all away from me, Life,
But I will not give up
My steadfastness.

❧ Hazard

I LIVED on an island
But now I have left
The shores that moulded
Then bounded me,
The air that braced
Then choked me,
The bonds that linked
Then snared me,
The fire that warmed
Then burnt me.

I have set sail
On an uncharted course,
Lacking strength to steer
And light to guide me
Across the rough seas
With sucking whirlpools
And lashing waves.
Storm-tossed I cannot
Navigate my boat
About to capsize.

I look up and see
Revealed by darkness
What the day concealed,
The Pole Star resplendent.

𝒳 A Wayfarer Enquires

My journey's direction
    Was long ago decided
By those who no more walk
    In company with me.

This once broad avenue
    Grows narrow for my feet
And closed-in overhead:
    How can I widen it?

Choice trees lining the way,
    Though tended caringly,
Have yielded bitter fruit:
    Why should this be so?

No chance to retrace steps
    Or take another route;
Onward, only onward:
    Where does the road lead?

... and Receives Replies

Take an axe and cut away
    The growth that hems you in.

The bitter fruit is medicine
    To ensure future health.

The road leads upwards
    To your true homeland.

❧ 'She Stole My Heart Away'

[English folk-song refrain]

"Many teachers steal away a student's means;
A teacher rare on earth steals a student's heart."

[Sanskrit adage]

THIRSTY FOR KNOWLEDGE, I was guided to you
And I came to drink at the well of your mind.
As I drank sip by sip the taste of the water
So limpid, so sweet, and offered so freely,
I experienced as nectar, sustaining to me.

Deep the well,
Sparkling the water,
Unslaked the thirst;
Long be the draught.

THE AUTHOR of the novel *Life*
Sent it for consideration
To a House of Publishing.

The Editor assigned to it
Corrected punctuation –
    Inserting proper pauses
        For rhythm and readability,
    Changing question marks of doubt
        Into stops of certainty;

Improved the syntax –
    Rewriting muddled sentences
        To make the meaning clear,
    Finishing unfinished lines
        To tidy up loose ends;

Altered the plot –
    Simplifying relationships
        For clarity and neatness,
    Moderating the fantastic
        With a view to realism;

Rationalised the structure –
    Reordering scenes
        For continuity of thought and action,
    Clustering all minor themes
        Around a major one;

Paced the action –
    Condensing humdrum interludes
        If they could not be excised,
    Dramatising happenings
        For maximum effect;

Redrew the characters –
    Recontouring personalities
        By psycho-plastic surgery,
    Adding and subtracting roles
        As convenient to the plot;

Polished the style –
    Replacing words
        To make scintillating prose,
    Avoiding repetition
        And thus the boredom factor;

Rewrote the ending –
    Suggesting an alternative
        According to prevailing taste,
    Drawing everything
        To a satisfactory conclusion;

And returned it to the Author
With Compliments.

✑ SURREAL BANQUET

THE TABLEAU is a table
    Laid with a sumptuous spread:
Luscious sweets and bonbons
    Laced with bitter herbs,
Plain and fancy savouries
    With piquant garnishes,
Relishes of acid sharpness
    Or puckering astringency;
The revellers are seated
    And the pageant starts.

The host, dressed as a jester,
    Serves haphazardly
Minute and giant portions,
    Jumbles courses, offers dishes,
Then whisks them away;
    The guests, in fetters,
Are constrained to eat (or not)
    According to his whims,
Without pause for breath,
    And may not leave the table.

Some foolish ones with envy
    Eye another's share;
But fortune's favourite
    To whom is given
A repast that satisfies
    May have as dessert
Unpalatable fare,
    And someone starving
May unexpectedly
    Receive a plate of plenty.

The mix of sounds
  Accompanying this scene
Produce both harmony and discord:
  Plaintive wails of hunger,
Sighs of satisfaction,
  Gasps of surprise
And disappointed moans,
  Conversation, altercation,
Munching, crunching;
  A menagerie of noise.

At this strange feast
  With its lottery of dishes
The diners must discover,
  Through silence in cacophony,
The recipe of each concoction
  And the menus set before them,
In order to divine the game
  And depart replete and free.

Gentle viewer, do not scoff,
For you are at this banquet too.

Beware
The cancer darkly growing,
Preying slowly on its host,
Sucking life out drop by drop.

Beware
Its power, fatal, creeping,
Seeping sickness into tissues,
Crumbling health into decay.

Beware
Its vice-like tightening,
Imprisoning and choking breath,
Bringing death by strangulation.

Cut! It must be cut,
Or there will be dying, dying.

Weigh up
Sleeping trauma's waking,
Frightening all with fearing face,
Needing speedy, calm attention.

Trust in
Benign fingers snipping,
Searching out malignancy,
Incising skin to excise threat.

Draw on
Faith and prayers for curing,
Reinforcing loving care,
Wishing wellness full and fast.

Healed! Let all be healed,
For the sake of living, living.

✑ Can the Stars Lie?

Prisoner
MY END I see,
Condemned to die
By guillotine
On a treason charge.

Chorus
TAKE HEART, Hero,
For you are blessed
With two lives
Within this mortal one.

Make freedom's plea
Your last request,
And it may be granted
With graciousness.

Boldly venture
To pastures new,
Where a bright star beckons
With clear, sure beam.

Life awaits you,
Not death just yet,
And laurels and plaudits
In Truth's good time.

Take heart, Hero,
For you are blessed
With two lives
Within this mortal one.

[*Inspired by Charles Dickens'* A Tale of Two Cities]

℘ WHEN IN DOUBT ...

LIFE, in a quandary
At a crossroads without signposts,
Knocked for advice nearby
At the house of a famous judge.

Two brothers were residing there,
Named the same by different mothers:
Wisdom, born of Adversity,
And Wisdom, Happy-Comfort's son.

Each opined with sense and vigour –
But gave conflicting views,
So Life, keeping her own counsel,
Wended her way herself.

RESPONSES

❧ To a Child Grown Up

See the colour of the sky!
Paint it with your inner eye!
Paint the trees, the sun, the flowers;
Choose your subject as you will,
But be true,
For if you cover
Night's dark shade with silver hue
Or the frankness or the beauty,
You will be the loser,
You.

❦ Eye Contact with Reality

Stand resolute and dare
To look reality in the eye;
Do not shade yours
Or avert your gaze,
Or let dreams
Becloud your vision,
Or use a tinted or distorting lens,
Or hide behind a veil
From its glare:

And that stern eye,
Encountering yours,
Will indicate by glances
Sidelong or direct,
And then, outstared,
By winks and twinkling
The clear, sure road
On which your sight is set
And smile.

❧ Scene by Flashlight

A SMILE'S bright flare
Illumines a face ...
And in a flash reveals,
Recessed behind composure,
   The shadow of care.

Words are the kindling;
Eyes see the hidden;
Love forms a prayer:
May lightness of heart
   Ever light up that smile.

✢ DANCE DIVINE

AN INVISIBLE band
    Plays inaudible strains.
Enter two dancers;
    They step, figure and twirl
       To natural time.

Side by side or in tandem,
    Now solo, now pairing,
They take it in turns
    To lead and to follow
       Exactly on cue.

Sure-footed and nimble,
    And foil to each other,
They tread their design;
    Their joy is their movement,
       Their ballet their grace.

❧ TIME-SHARING

I HAVE a timepiece
　　With a handsome face
But whose springs are gone,
　　And whose tick-tock slows
And slows
　　To a stop.

I see that your clock's dial is dimmed
　　But its wheels and cogs turn smoothly.
Shall we put the two together
　　To make one perfect instrument
With bright clear look
　　And well-timed chimes?

❧ WORD STREAMS

LIKE A FLOWING STREAM your words
Beside which I sit
And scoop the water with hollowed palms,
Or sometimes spread my fingers with delight
To see it trickling, coruscating,
And my hands glistening and wet,
Or watch the gently rolling ripples
Glide across the surface,
Stirred by thoughts from deep within
Or breeze-blown from outside.

My hands too small to hold
The vastness of the flow
That reaches back to farthest time,
I will plunge in, immerse myself,
To feel its powerful embrace
Envelop and carry me exhilarated onward,
Fearless of drowning, and with confidence absolute
In the harmony of conjoining currents,
For I too am a stream of words
Irrepressibly pouring.

✧ MOVING WORDS

SIR,

So charming your missive of elegant couplets,
No shadow discernible in their perfection
Of the desuetude lamented of a proud skill!

With great pleasure I see your art in composing
Thoughts measured by metre in a language of yore,
Whose structure and beauty I struggle to master.

In like fashion I answer, but one thing I rue:
The instruments of my epistolary style
Are chained to their neighbours, lacking freedom to rove.

A BEGGAR accosted
A lady in silk,
Voice rasping and urgent,
"Give me your love."

In alarm she stepped back
And clasped her purse close.
"I beg you for kindness;
Please do me no harm.

"I live on my honour,
I speak only truth,
I am without anger
Or meanness or greed."

The beggar drew nearer
And clutched at her sleeve.
"Virtue is luxury
I can't afford.

"Have you felt hunger,
Have you felt cold,
Have you fought grimly
The world as your foe?

"Have you felt hatred,
Have you felt rage,
Have you felt cheated
And beaten by Fate?"

"No," whispered the lady,
Averting her face,
And, opening her wallet,
She took out a coin.

"Go home to your comforts
And cupboards well stocked,
Your children around you,
And laughter and cheer.

"In your pious prayers
Tonight by your bed
Give thanks to your Maker
That you are not I."

〇 WEIGHINGS

ALONG THE SUN-SEARED road barefoot,
Grey-faced and bowed, the carter drags
His heavy load with heavy step.

Who is the guilty one?

He: for he shoulders just
The burden of past sins

(So deems the law that draws
Just consequence to deed);

Or I: who, insouciant
And innocent of toil,

Ride by and fail to stop.

Pain is not bound to poverty:
Free as a bird, at will it lights,
Then masses its weight like a stone.

✗ A Hitch in Matchmaking

Peopled with Questions
Of all races and hues
    Is the realm of my mind;
Eagerly they queue
With presentation speech
    To meet their Replies.

But when the Master of Answers
Arrives with his men,
    Word-forgotten, they flee,
For he floods
The whole domain
    With quietness.

A MERRY CHESS LESSON

GRANDMASTER Circumstance,
  Full of ploys and tricks
To test his pupils' wits
  Against his whimsy,

Hiccups

  And disarrays the board.
With grit the learners
  Re-marshal their forces,
And he applauds and

Sneezes.

SENTIMENTS

Xo

༄ Mawkish vs Unsentimental

The defendant, Sir Unsentimental,
In deliberate contravention
Of regulations governing
Commemorative transactions,
Opened his birthday present
Before the due date,
Claiming indifference to anniversaries
Owing to a mature mind.

The Plaintiff, Ms Mawkish,
A strict adherent of custom,
Believing the said profession
A pretext concealing eagerness
To view the aforementioned object,
And the deed having taken place
So far in advance of the day
As to negate the significance
Of their particular connection,
Felt obliged thereby
To procure for him a replacement
To mark the occasion,
And therefore asks to be awarded
Appropriate compensation.

The Court finds against the Defendant
And orders him to pay damages
Of one hundred _____ .

✐ SILKEN STRINGS

JEALOUSY
Binds its object with tight cords,
Draws it in a close embrace
And strangles it,
Or ties it to a stake
To set it ablaze.

Love
Binds its object with gossamer,
Lets it roam at will
And puts in its hand
The end of the thread
To clue the way home.

℀ GLAD RAGS

ON THE RAIL hang gowns of gladness
In all modes and shades.
Hold them to you, feel their fabric,
Try them on for size:

Communion in comradeship,
The transport of bliss,
Satisfaction through fulfilment,
Contentment with your lot,
Blithe ignorance, light-hearted glee,
Calm beatitude.

If what you seek is not in stock
Do not grow too glum;
Wait patiently to see unveiled
Next season's chic designs:
For sure amongst them there will be
Just the one for you.

If it needs pins, tucks and stitches,
Keep an open mind:
Alteration may become you
Perfectly and better
Than the best of all your dreams.
Wear it jauntily.

✑ THAT FOOL HOPE

IN A DROUGHT-RIDDEN land
Hope springs up like a seed
At the fancy of rain
And, husbanded, burgeons ...

Till the sere stroke of fact
Blights the crop as it grows,
Yielding husks of despair,
A harvest of famine;

Still the starveling farmer
Calls on Fate to provide.

... FINDS LIGHT RELIEF

TO SIT in a meadow
Surrounded by sunshine;
To wake from a nightmare
That gnawed at the bones.

The pure air reviving,
Spirit recovering;
After devouring eclipse,
To laugh in the light.

⁊ Outing to a Gallery of Betrayers

Look how the first portrait shows
Selfish indifference;

Examine the second face
For manic jealousy;

In the gentle third descry
Numb fear and cowardice;

And see how each neatly wears
The mask of piety.

❧ THE GOOD HOUSEKEEPER

Wʜᴏ ᴄᴀɴ stand up and say,

"My house is spick and span
And I have never walked
With dirty feet into another's;

"I have never whitewashed
Dark patches on my walls,
For there are none to hide;

"I have never eaten
My neighbour's fruit unbid
That drops into my garden;

"Nor have I moved the fence
That lies between our lands
Even a little bit."?

O, germ-free, guiltless Paragon,
What is the price of purity?

You must bolt all doors and windows
To shut pollution out,
And shun intercourse with others
Lest you catch their sin from them.

✐ ALL FOR ANOTHER

A WEAVER SHOT shuttle
   Forward and back, skein after skein,
To make a shawl of soft, fine wool.

A deft embroideress
   Stitched round it an exquisite edge
Vibrant with rainbow-coloured silks.

A market-shrewd merchant
   Aesthetically displayed it
To attract the eye of patrons.

A man searching bought it
   For its quality workmanship
As a celebratory gift.

A pleased, laughing lady
   Enjoyed its light, versatile warmth:
Wrap by day, coverlet by night.

❡ DISARMING ARM

A SWORDSMITH forges
With learning's hammer
On wanting's anvil

A sword of wisdom

Mind-sharpened
Will-tempered
Wit-polished

And sheathes it in peace

For its knowledge blade
Is keener than steel
And its thrust unerring.

℀ BEGONE, FEAR!

CHALLENGED, the demon Fear
Gnashes its teeth in rage
And makes a show of might:
Wild-eyed, it cracks its whip,
Threatens with spike-gloved fist
And chills the spine with roars.

But the sorcerer's spell
Is undone by the bold;
Terror-struck at death's knell
The usurper cries craven
And, wraith-faint, cedes the throne
To its ruler by right.

❧ Good Luck, My Son

"Where does Luck live, Mother?
I want to go find him."
"Nowhere and anywhere,
Nobody knows." "Surely,
If he exists, Mother,
He must live somewhere."

"Since you are determined,
You must be clever;
To catch Luck's quicksilver
Use perseverance,
And never be reckless
Or gamble when lost.

"Seek him in all corners,
Even unlikely,
Ask all you encounter
How to detect him,
Know all his disguises,
For he may be she.

"As he zigzag meanders
Stalk him like a shadow,
Steal up on him swiftly
Then, at a judged second,
Grasp him by the shoulder,
Greet him and – please him."

℘ SCHERZO

LUCK IN LOVE after carousing
Too much took a draught
To fall sleeping and slumbered
Too long; he awoke
With a start, leapt out of bed
In a hurry and kissed
Whomsoever he met.

REFLECTIONS

❧ THE EDGE OF GENTLENESS

Diamond hardness
Cuts diamond;
But it is gentleness
That smooths away
Sharp edges.

Diamond hardness
Cuts diamond;
But refining's gentle touch
Makes its edges
Razor-sharp.

A BROKEN bell
Mutely lies.

Make the halves whole
And their voice, become one,
Rings out
Pure and true.

Now the silence of the bell
Is a prelude to its pealing:

Note after note
    Into bar after bar
        Into tune after tune
Sounds and lingers in the air,

Music for the ear,
    Elation for the mind,
        Entrancement for the heart,
Harmonics for the soul.

℘ SILENCING SILENCE

LIKE A MANTLE silence covers,
Like a gag it seals and stifles,
Like a noose it squeezes speechless,
Like a fog it mystifies.

Like laryngitis it allows
Escape to muteness with excuse
Whereby the listener is let
Imagine or construe at will.

Like a coward struck with dumbness
At the mere thought of consequence
To life and limb, it passively
Lets duty pass it by undone.

Like an artful politician
It evades or ignores questions
Testing probity or purpose,
Glibly eliding commitment.

Call the clarion voice of conscience
To rend the shroud cast over it,
Unstop lips, loosen constriction
 And remove ambiguousness.

Take a sip of soothing linctus
To ease the throat for words to pass;
Exhort the coward to be brave
To act in rightness without fear;
Catch the wily politician
And make him speak the truth.

MANY ARE the routes to Truth,
 That unfailing, glowing globe
Which draws heart and mind to bathe
 In its candent, candid light;
Yet though often known and straight,
 None is easy to traverse.

The journey of the seeker
 May lie through tangled jungle
Overgrown with time and stealth,
 Across high, forbidding crags
Or trackless, barren desert
 Misleading to mirages.

Icy winds may kiss and bribe
 Footpaths into treachery,
Snipers may in hiding wait
 Along pleasant, open roads,
And darkness render scary
 Narrow, unfrequented lanes.

Yet no byway is untrod,
 And the walker who sets out
With candour for a lantern
 Will find to hand when needed
Staff and knife and thick-lined cloak,
 And will surely reach the goal.

℀ CREDO

TYRANNICAL belief,
That compels through fear
Action or inaction,
Enthralling emasculated
    The power of judgement.

The belief of faith,
Blind as those are blind
Who do not wish to see,
Or, inured by habit,
    Fail in noticing.

Persuasive belief,
Lapped up from flattery,
Whose syrup tongue
Imparts congenial views
    So unctuous sweet.

The belief in truth,
Demanding evidence
And its brave and careful weighing,
Whereby are satisfied
    Intellect and conscience.

Sustaining belief,
In goodness or duty,
In God or a cause,
In oneself or another,
    That gives purpose to life.

❀ TURNING THE TABLES

I INTRODUCE my smiling maid:
Dishes galore with flair she cooks,
Cleans the rooms with vim and vigour
Like a cheerful house-proud housewife
And rearranges furniture
To give a new look to the old.
We chat in our respective tongues,
Criss-crossing meanings now and then;
Mutual affection nurtured grows.

One day, shocked and dismayed, I find
A lock picked and my money gone:
No one but she can be the thief.
Confronted, she is brazen, bold,
With eyes impenetrably veiled;
Her loud denials silently
Accuse me ... I am half amused
And I admire her defiance;
Her mute attack has vanquished me.

How can I judge her right and wrong?
I do not have a drunkard son,
A husband sick in hospital
Or grandchildren to send to school.
I do not possess no learning
Nor no recourse except my hands;
I do not have so many things.
What would I do to find the fees
If I were her? I do not know.

✠ GHOSTS HAUNT A QUEEN

[Queen Vaasavadattaa,
Falsely proclaimed as dead
To enable the King
To remarry to save
The kingdom from warfare –
A stratagem advised
By the King's councillor –
Appears to her husband
In a dream.]

NOT ALL my ghosts as yet
Are exorcised; they haunt
The leaves of books I read
With eerie cries and twist
With warpèd tongues and hissing
Whispers the stories of my childhood
Innocence, so now I cannot
View the scheming minister except
With eyes in succession wet and
Whetted by the wily
Hypocrisy of those close by
Me who wear the garb
Of righteous action, nor see the witless
King without contempt, for
Witless is not guileless, nor
Regard the woman
Victimised without the parallel
Of life where cruelty
Abounds, and I wonder
At the conceptualising mind and
The admiring audience who make
Faults virtues.

[Note: Svapnavaasavadatta, 'Dream Vaasavadattaa'
is a 2000-year-old Sanskrit drama by Bhaasha.]

✣ WEIGHTLESS PRESSURE

THE HEAVINESS
Of absence
Presses down
On life
And crushes it to
                    death.

Amazing how
Non-existence
Weighs so much
And kills
The substance of
                    existence.

❧ NEVER SAY DIE

SOMETIMES Wisdom for the way ahead
Needs a lamp to see by
And a stick to lean on
To help it find its path,
Lest it falter, not through fear,
But from a taxed, taxed dry endurance,
At the stark straitness of the pass.

Let it remember then
A mother's loving arms and care
And endlessly supporting strength.

✑ HARLEQUINADE

I, HARLEQUIN, ride
   A large bouncy ball,
Make motions of walking
   To stay where I am;
My paint mask expresses
   Now happy, now sad.

Quick as lightning my hands
   Gesture for balance
And toss and catch skittles
   I trace with my eyes;
My mind's occupation,
   Success in my act.

What chance in this circus
   To be the real me?
I am not my disguise
   Nor my juggler's tricks –
Or am I fit only
   For pantomime skits?

Backstage it is quiet,
   The dressing room lit;
The show will continue
   With or without me;
To uncostume myself
   I need merely jump off.

AFTER A HAIKU

FAREWELL bids enter
 Shy new beginning: leaves bow
  To fresh growth's curtsey.

TALES AND FABLES

❧ Magic in the Air

Inquisitive I,

For I, by fortune bidden, meet
A wandering thaumaturge
Who favours me with a display
Of her wonder-working art.

With potent spells
She unlooses chafing chains;
By sleight of hand
She makes troubles disappear;
She waves her sparking wizard's wand
And oh!
A sweet fresh breeze blows
And light engulfs the dark;
Her handclap
Conjures smiling joyousness
In all directions
Out of empty space.

In the twinkling of an eye
Incredulous I
Becomes
Inspired I,
Envisioning a world
Boundless with freedom,
Beaconed with laughter,
Benisoned with peace.

Indebted I.

ℒ THE TOY-MAKER'S ARTIFICE

A TOY-MAKER with artful craft
    And a sense of humour
Fashioned a pair of minstrel dolls,
    A singer and a lutist.

He gave the singer a song-scroll
    Adorned with wiseness pearls
And a fine filigree of wit;
    But he sealed her lips.

An instrument with resonance
    And purity of tone
He placed in the lute-player's hands;
    But he did not give it strings.

He made their limbs articulate
    And breathed into their mouths
To rouse them to animation;
    Then he challenged them:

"I have made you to make music
    And given you rare gifts,
But you must solve the puzzle first
    Of how you can play and sing."

From her jewelled scroll the singer
    Wrought a set of strings, when
To unseal her lips the lutist
    Set on them a kiss.

ᴑ FINDERS KEEPERS?

A PRECIOUS DIADEM, so the story goes,
Fell somehow from the head-dress of a nymph.
Lacklustre from its loss, and disconsolate,
She wandered far and wide in search of it.

In a distant land the coronet was found
By a cutter of gems, who polished it
And gave it pride of place in his collection;
But slowly its ethereal brightness dimmed.

One day the nymph happened on this jeweller
And recognised her crown; she claimed it back.
First refusing, then reluctant, he at last
In generous spirit relinquished it.

Thus were gem-band and damsel reunited,
And each enhanced the other's radiance.

❧ SERENDIPITIES

A RESTLESS water-sprite
Left her river dwelling
And wandered far upstream,
Seeking adventure and new sights.

She clambered to a cleft
In a high rock fastness
And came upon a cave
Enchanting and unoccupied.

Exploring everywhere,
She let air currents in,
Testing its ambience,
She hung the walls with spangled shells.

A faint rumble calling
From a distant corner,
She discovered covered
By stones and moss a gurgling stream.

Unblocked, it tumbled out,
And, skipping in, she found
Her true home a well-spring
Bubbling fresh from the mountain's core.

✑ FISH FANTASY

AN EAGLE soared
And spied a lake,
And dived deep down
Into its heart;
There it became
A flying fish
With golden fins.

It grew and grew
And drank the lake ...

From there it flew
Into the sea
Whose vast expanse,
And sky above,
Gave space for its
Majestic size
And height of flight.

❧ The King is in His Castle

A SPECULATOR skilled in restoration,
Intrigued by a property
Espied upon his journeying,
Approached the agent for the key.

Cutting through dense undergrowth,
He unlocked the door and entered.
He found the house in poor repair
And circumfused with gloom.

But it had potential,
And so he set to work:

He flung the windows open
To let the sunlight in;
He took down the curtains
Blotched and musty with despair;
He swept and washed the floors
Thick with dust from crumbled hopes;
He painted all the walls
Stained with floods of tears;
He made good the crack
Which split the hearth in two.

Next, tastefully, and piece by piece,
He furnished it with fine effects.

Finding now its aspect charming,
Comfort in its chambers,
And its value soared to priceless,
He himself moved in.

℘ The Price of Dust

A CURATOR of the Museum of Ideas
Perused catalogues keenly, bent on acquiring
Prize possessions to display in the showcase,
New Insights and Mature Understanding.

Preoccupied with the purchase of his collection,
Alas! he neglected to pay his assistant,
And obliged him to find employment elsewhere.
Thus the exhibits, unseen, gathered dust.

⌘ On Land and At Sea

A MERMAID fell in love
With a handsome merman;
The two swam happily
In a secluded pool.

The merman suffered now and then
From a strange complaint: a tail itch,
Which was relieved when scratched and thus,
Although not cured, could be ignored.

One day the itch was so intense
He found no ease, but twitched and thrashed
Until his tail split into two –
Transforming merman into man.

How the little mermaid sobbed!
Her heart was rent, just like the tail.
But what to do, or could be done?
Who can bear another's pain?

ℐ The Pomegranate Expert

An orbèd casket stowed
A cache of ruby drops.
Covetous, and tools in hand,
A jewel thief came by
And with dextrous nonchalance
Sliced off the lid,
Quarter-scored the box,
Prised with taloned fingers
Its four compartments open
And, unpacking swiftly
The treasure trove of gems,
Secreted all away.

℘ It Began with an Ambush

Listen to this old debate
On the rise of a simple boy:

In his land a band of brigands
Terrorized the highway
To the city of the Queen;
They purposed burglary of wealth
Earned by others with travail.

One day the boy traversed this road
To pay his annual taxes;
He was set upon, surprised,
And was tied and gagged and dragged
To a deserted spot as dead.

Reconnoitring for survival,
The boy chanced upon the hut
Of a master forester
Who salved and bound his wounds
And took him as apprentice.

For seven years he studied
The lore of trees and plants;
He practised on a reed-pipe
The subtle scales and chords
Attuned to their vibrations.

A maestro now, he travelled home
And crossed the infested road;
With magic pipe he charmed the trees ...
Which one by one pulled up their roots
And followed him like sheep.

They formed themselves into a copse,
A shelter from the burning sun.
The denuded roadside offered
No hideout now for robbers
To ply their nefarious trade.

Saved from danger and oppression,
Full of gratitude and joy,
Queen and people praised the boy,
Showered him with gifts and blessings
And crowned him the next King.

Now, was the cause of his success
His constant will or the caprice
Of schizophrenic Fate?

℀ To Bottle the Genie

THE JAR of the Genie, once unstoppered,
  Released its pent spirit, which expanded
    Exponentially upwards and outwards
      Into freedom co-terminous with space.

        No coercion, cajoling or trickery
      Could return the escapee to confinement;
    But were the air sucked out of its sky-room
  Would it not shrink back in the vacuum?

TIME AND MIND

Ꭷ Two Chameleons

The chameleon Time
Alters
According to the context of the mind
Which gives it
Fleet or laggard markings.

The chameleon Mind
Modifies
The hue of words and deeds intended
To match
The setting of the present.

ᗡ Eternal Conundrum

LONELY Time, to while away the hours,
Fashions a game of moving pieces
Set upon a board that shakes and tips
In turn each one whose play is over
Into Space from which he conjured it.

He constructs round each a changing scene
Of locations and relationships
And, using his creator's power,
Implants in each a separate will
According to which it interacts.

But once this game is set in motion
It poses Time its own conundrum,
Challenging him to give the answer:
Are the moves and motives of each piece
Autonomous or pre-determined?

℘ TANTALISING TWINKLES

WHAT FUN it is to tease:
To watch perplexity
And answer-striving thoughts
Flit across another's face
Along the avenues of disposition
And on paths as yet untrod
In essays at divination.

How wonderful the compass of the mind,
Whose illimitable reach
Can plumb the depths and climb the heights
Of abstruse ideation
And set its course at will
In known or new directions,
Logging intricate instructions
To chart the terrain explored.

Still greater marvel,
The uniqueness of each instrument
Whereby none can know another's thought
Except by tell-tale signs or telling.

And yet the mind,
For all its vast capacity
To swallow all the world and more,
Is satisfied by something small.

Hence the attraction of the guess:
The delight on seeing
Delight on seeing
An unimaginable gift:
A picture of sequins.

✗ THOUGHT-PLANES

THOUGHT-PLANES hover and circle
Above the busy city;
Can't you see their wings? Look hard!

They are cleverly designed
With ample seats and storage
To accommodate all kinds
Of adventurers and freight,
And yet their shape is streamlined.

Their speed is supersonic,
And they easily perform
Amazing acrobatic feats:
Climbs, nose-dives, sideways flying,
Zigzags, loops and figure eights.

A landing space is signalled
By the traffic controller;
Descending through the clouds,
They skim along the runway
And halt at the thought-port gates.

They wait for the loudspeaker
Announcement of their presence
And then they take off again.

Hurry! Do not miss the plane!

❧ Figurative Flight

Like a kite imagination floats
    This way and that in the breeze of fancy,
Or stays becalmed in picture-clouds,
    Or soars and tumbles in gusty gales
That send its figments spinning
    Into whirlwinds of fantasy.

Thick or thin a thread ties it
    And links it to a hand, the mind,
And marks a limit to its flight,
    Beyond which boundary envisaging,
Held by the leash experience,
    Does not stray of its own accord.

But another's steering makes it fly
    Across the frontiers of proclivity
Over new lands of imaging
    Which seed conception of the unconceived:
The attachment of a boy
    To his first beard.

↗ THE SIFTINGS OF TIME

SO MANY THINGS unsaid,
For the sieve of time,
With relentless rhythm tapped,
Lets fall the small
And retains the great.

But who is to say
That smallness
Is inconsequent,
Or that words unspoken
Die buried by silence?

❧ THE CONQUEROR'S CAUSEWAY

THOUGHT, that ingenious device
By which all boundaries are set at nought,
Commanded by the Thinker
To span the struts of days and distance
Measured invisibly by missing,
Constructs bridges of brush strokes
And promenades with words for cobblestones,
Lanterning them with meaning:

Thus is time paved
And space bestridden
By Mind the Conqueror.

✺ A Sanskrit Poser

"ANUSHTUBH stanzas are composed
Of eight syllables and four feet.
I doubt if you, a novice, can
Capture this catchy metre's beat."

या शिष्या चिरमन्विष्टा
त्वया त्वां प्राप सा चिरात् ।

yaa shishyaa chiramanvishtaa
tvayaa tvaam praapa saa chiraat.

She who was sought so long by you
As pupil has found you at last.

❦ Ocean Waves

Skin against skin:
The thrill of the soft caress,
A common tangency.

Mind against mind:
A rare contiguity,
But oh, the joy of the touch!

Two currents
Undulating into one,
Ripple after ripple
Welling, swelling and subsiding
Within a soundless deep.

✐ ON TICKLING

SUCH A TICKLISH topic!

My poor brain reels
From the effort of stretching
And pulling my mind
Over hills and round corners
To places unvisited
For a very long time.

My search for an answer
Is proving a tickler;
But I hope my essay
Will tickle your fancy:

Definition
Eureka! In thumbing through
A directory of the Anglo-Saxon tongue
I came across, at its initial opening,
"Thigmotropism", a Greek concoction signifying
"Response to stimulus of touch".

Elucidation
Thus to tickle is to excite
A thigmotropic reaction;
Just as the trigger for all other senses
Is an external object, so also is another
The arouser for tactility.

Conclusion
The sum and substance of this thesis:
The coupling of skill and thrill
As subtle tactile interplay;
Its wider purpose, to give purring pleasure.
May one and all be tickled pink!

NATURE

𝒴 UTTER WONDER

HOW THE SEEDS dormant through the dark Winter
Awaken and struggle through the dark Earth
Into the light on the first day of Spring!

℘ PAINTING MASTER CLASS

How does the Creator
Make his world so gorgeous,
Moving soul and senses?

He is at his easel,
Blending tints from rainbows,
Crooning as he sketches.

Let us tiptoe closer,
Peep across his shoulder,
Eavesdrop on his secrets ...

Use seven pencils, thin to thick,
With seven pressures, faint to strong,
In seven shade-tones, light to dark,
On seven layers, base to top.

Measure breadth and length, and, squinting,
Mix and match the magic numbers,
Rub over with a soft white cloth
To daub in the lights and highlights.

See now! By sure strokes, step by step,
A form takes shape, then depth, then life.

✗ Horizon's Cup

WHAT CAN contain
The broad expanse of earth and sky
With clouds and tree-clad hills,
Path-crossed fields and habitations
And birds a-flitting,
    A landscape stretching to infinity?

Only a deep-bowled lake,
Which quaffs it as a draught
To quench its thirst,
Then, brimmed and satisfied, holds still
The imbibition and to it adds
    The sparkle of the sun.

... AND DRINKER'S FILL

WHAT CAN gratify a deep-bowled lake?
Only the broad expanse of earth and sky ...

℘ Heavenly Bodies

Its gold brings gladness
To quell sadness,
And warmth and cheer
To banish fear.

Their silver shimmer
Set against a shade of night
Beautifies the day.

✗ TWILIGHTS

MISTS ARE swirling
And their thickness
Muffles the distant piper's tune
In the penumbra of the dawn.

The drum of time
Rolls gloom away
And clearly sounds the melody
That beckons day to follow it.

Darkness passing
Trails its shadow
In its wake;
Though morning comes

Sunbeams streaming
Do not dispel
From deepest depths
The scent of night.

✒ THUNDER STORM

IN THE SKY the storm clouds lour
Dark, foreboding frenzied spate:

Rolling roars and jagging light,
Stunning ears and blinding eyes,
Are harbingers of sheeting streams
Pounding ground and roofs and heads,
Drenching cowering birds and beasts,
Lashing stillness from the lakes.

Spent its fury come the morning;
Unknown yet its aftermath:
Mired waters, ravaged earth, or
Bright world purged of turbulence.

⌀ PATHOGENESIS

SOMETIMES within Nature's plan

An organism flourishes
In the full fresh flush of youth
And prime of maturity,

Paying no heed to prodromes
That seem, although recurrent,
So slight and little troubling,

Till there suddenly erupts
A grave malady that shows
That the while a fatal growth

Was producing tentacles
Which gripped health by the throttle
And left in its stead a trail

Of ugly death and ruin.

✎ BLAZE

THE AIR is numbing chill,
Bitter to the marrow.

Rub, rub begrudging flint
Against unyielding steel
Till friction sparks fly fanned
Inflaming tinder laid.

Ah! Warm your hands and watch
As the fire scorches, burns.

Oh! Fend off peril where
Conflagration's passion,
Smouldering, ravening,
Stokes itself with you.

✑ BIO-MAGNETISM

ACCORDING TO the Law of Magnets
The operation of a pole
Is only a relation to its counterpart,
The two obedient to a hidden force
That both binds and separates them.

Thus a pole appears autonomous
In its own vicinity
Until its opposite,
So remote in space and travel-time
As to seem non-existent,
Is motivated to impinge on it;
Then the energy between them
Aligns the elements that lie
Within its linking field.

Applying polarity to life,
The same holds true:

In conducive circumstance
Attraction manifest is irresistible,
And its harmonising power
Choreographs the scattered parts
That seemed before unpurposed
Into a synergetic ballet,
As splinters of iron
Dance in formation
To the tune of the lodestone.

✕ NOCTURNE

THROUGH WHAT perils does Dawn travel
With hushed footfall stealthily
In the labyrinth of Night,
Leading Daylight by the hand
Cowled in blackness for disguise
To the exit of the maze,
Where she holds her lamp aloft
And lights the progress of the Day?

❧ Moonshine

Last night I had a visit from the Moon.
I asked the reason why she waxed and waned.

I parallel the course of human hearts (she said):
When held in my beloved's gaze, I glow;

When he is cold and distant, I decline
And fade to unrequited emptiness.

Yet I forgive him for deserting me;
He just obeys his orbit, as do I.

His smile upon my visage makes me beam
First shyly, then more broadly by degrees

Till I am wholly luminous again
With my own lustre, not a counterfeit.

Thus I do not reflect inconstancy
But the appointed rule of lovers' ways.

LIFE AND DEATH
THE TREE

❧ Symbiosis

CURIOSITY asks
In an idle moment
Why the verdant creeper
Clings to the hoary tree,
Twining round about it,
Pliant yet tenacious.

The sturdy tree
Carries the Earth's wide wisdom
Imbibed through deep roots
In all directions probing;
Its stance is straight,
But its boughs grow bowed
With the weight of its knowing
And sigh in the wind;
Its rustling leaves
Leave a sweet scent in the air,
But its sap runs dry.

Ah! But the dainty creeper
Feeds on its plenty,
And lightens its load;
Drinks of its essence,
And restores its fading splendour;
Climbs athwart its bulk,
And injects it with fresh growth;
Coiling tendrils,
Hung as if with floral beads
Along a leafy helix,
Grafted onto mottled trunk.

Life sustaining life;
Is there a purpose
External to each?
Is it to create
A lasting vision
For the eye and mind?

❧ THE DESIGN OF CHANCE

WINDWARD swept
By chance and circumstance
Into the lee
Of its natural support,
The creeper basks
In the living of the tree
And blooms in its shelter
With embrace.

✑ PERPETUATION

Is the tree so fixed
In its accustomed habitat
That daily grows jejune,

Or can it bow
To the winds of change
That strongly blow

And venture shoots
In pioneer directions
Where new need beckons,

To bear its fruits
Ripened to succulence
For other connoisseurs

And strew its seeds
In fertile untilled ground?

❧ THE BIRD ON THE BRANCH

AH! WISE TREE, sings the bird,

Grow a new branch
With all your main,

And I will carry it
And plant it firm afar

Where it can show in time
Its majesty in full

Of mighty trunk
And leaves unfurled

Against wide open skies.

✑ STUMPED

PLANTED IN too small a space
The tree strains in vain to grow,
But its long roots short of soil,
Exposed, start to desiccate.

Plucked from its sustaining shade,
The creeper curls in a heap,
Life-drained, and begins to fade.

Growth's defeated forces
Call the retreat of Spring's advance
To the Winter of surrender.

❧ THE SHAKEN TREE

Is it the wind that shakes the tree
(Or the creeper by its twining
That rocks it with insistent force)

And sways its years of rootedness
Towards transplanting in a soil
Where its fruit can grow to ripeness?

In its birthplace it is stunted,
But when re-rooted will it thrive?

✑ REVIVAL

A LOG LOPPED from a tree
Rolled into the sea
And floated awhile

Till the swell of the tide
Propelled it ashore

To a land where the clime,
So suiting its frame,
Caused it to put forth
New roots and new shoots
In a wonder of life.

GROWTH
AND CULTIVATION
THE GARDENER AND
THE GARDEN

℘ BLUEPRINT FOR A GARDEN

YOU MUST BE a gardener:
Select your seeds with care,
Mark how they spread roots
And grow into a host of plants,
Luxuriant with foliage
Or riotous with blooms.

Create from them a pleasure ground,
With here and there a shady grove,
A rockery, a pergola,
A wondrous cactus show.
Chiaroscuro, form and texture:
Be an artist using nature's palette.

Delighting in this paradise,
Humming birds and honey bees
Will be darting to and fro,
Melodiously singing
Or sucking nectar from the blossoms;
You must catch their sweetness.

Make the garden's centrepiece
And life-sustaining source
A tranquil, vital lake,
Bestrewn with lotuses
And bordered by a grassy verge,
Enticing as a resting-place.

Signpost well this sculpted park
And cut paths towards the lake;
For those who gaze into its depths,
In the stillness of reflection,
Will see emerging slowly
The image of the tree of wisdom.

❧ MOSAIC MASTERPIECE

WITH EACH VERSE I pen
I place a stepping stone
Towards the future,
Across the river
Raging of the past,

And I cross to the far bank,
To the land marked for your garden.
I will help you plant it,
For in the soothing touch of flowers
And the balm of greenery
I can spend a peaceful present.

Your expert, innovative hand
Linked to my visionary's eye
Will create a timeless world,
Wherein humdrum horizons
Brighten to glorious vistas,
And poignant memories to glad.

Inscrutable in two existences,
Far-flung and as if at random shaped,
Time's purpose by their overlay
Stands now revealed: to make
A single interlocking pattern
Giving joy to the beholder.

✎ WATERFALL

PLOP!
I drop
Idea
And idea
Into your ear
And wait
For them
To percolate
Into your mind,
Pool there
And then
Debouch
Into a fresh
Clear spring,
The source
Of water
For your garden.

✑ A Tour of the Garden

IMAGINE ME beside you,
Take me gently by the hand
And show me round the garden
In whose ambience you grew
And where you shape your days.

Pick buds and flowers for me
To make into a nosegay,
Aromatic as I walk;
Cull for me a fine bouquet
For encircling with my arms.

Give me of each herb to taste,
Of each berry and each fruit,
And explain to me their use;
Wind a creeper in my hair
And weave me a fan of ferns.

Share with me the hidden glade
Where you sit and contemplate,
Where tall, close trees stand quiet guard,
Dappled light plays on the grass
And a soft breeze waves the leaves.

Stay by me at the lakeside
Where eye, ear and heart find rest;
Cup its water in your hands
And give me to drink and drink,
For my thirst is very great.

ℱ Forget-Me-Not

Sun and air and rain aplenty
Do not revive the ailing plant,
But the gardener, heedless, remiss,
Pays perfunctory attention,
Cocooned in busyness elsewhere.

Sun and air and rain aplenty
Will not heal the plant now dying;
Gone its spirit from the garden,
Its place replaced by emptiness.
What is the use of mourning?

℘ STRANGLE-WEED

BE CAREFUL, Gardener!
Do not sow the seeds of doubt
In the ground where trust grows greenly.

Once it takes root its tangles
Will defy eradication
And overrun the garden,

Destroying all the plants.

✗ METAMORPHOSIS

A RAVAGED WILDERNESS where grows
Nothing save a thorny thicket
    Piercing one who seeks its flowers:

A challenge to the gardener's skills,
To tame and coax wild nature
    Into gentle cultivation.

FREEDOM
AND CAPTIVITY
THE SONGBIRD

✎ HESITANT NOTE

THE SONGBIRD
Perches
In doubt
Upon the branch;

What
Will persuade it
To burst
Into song?

❦ THRENODY

THE SALT TEARS of the bird
Fall onto its tongue
And swamp its song's sweetness.

The scarred strings of its heart
Pull taut on its throat,
Tuned but to bitterness.

Wings weary of flying,
It pines for its mate
In a cold empty nest.

❧ The Songbird's Petition

The Prince of the Palace
  Found a sweet-throated songbird
And, captivated, captured it
  And hid it in his rooms.

Delighted with its warbling,
  He often stroked its plumage,
And for its food he stole
  Choice morsels from his table.

Yet hunger gnawed the bird
  And in anger based on trust
It demanded more to eat,
  And pondered its escape.

The Prince, himself well-fed,
  Not knowing hunger-pangs,
Refused, having naught to give
  Except from his own plate.

He assured it of his care
  And, bidding it be patient
For a fine feast to come,
  Chid it for selfishness.

The bird, contrite, resolved
  Resignation to its fate:
Clipped wings barred a life elsewhere
  And it trusted in the Prince.

But its voice would not be quelled
    And rose up from its throat:
"I am unsatisfied,
    You must give me more.

"You caught me and must keep me,
    You love me for my songs;
I am cut and captive caged –
    Will you also make me starve?

"Give me food to grow my wings
    And build strength to fly my cage;
Then I will sing aloud for you
    The song which tells your soul."

✑ PROPHECY

IN TIME'S fullness
The cagèd bird
        Will freely fly

And shed the gag
That binds its beak,
              And from its throat
              Will issue forth
                        Its song of truth.

ᴀ SHRILL KEY

LOOK! The cageling is parched with thirst
    (Sweet the drink in its cup but scant)
And its voice dries to a croak.

It flaps its wings against the bars
    (Gilded the cage, but still a jail),
Desperate for liberty:

The spanning skies, the radiant sun,
And the joy, the joys of its home
By a beauteous fountain.

Where is the key to the cage door?
    (Small though it be, it is not lost.)
Find it, and set the bird free!

❦ FLIGHT

THE PRINCE,
Careless of the bird,
Set it without the palace.

In the dark
A chance sharp edge
Cleft the cage

And it flew free.

TO A LOVER

xo

✗ THE STOPPING OF SPEECH

M Y EARS thrill to hold
   The cadence of your sounds;
My mind loves to touch
   The meaning of your words;
My lips want to stay
Your lips that convey
   Such stillness to my heart.

✤ Door to Daylight

Shall i tell you why I love you?
Because your face is gentle
And your eyes are kind,
Because inside you there is calmness
And your words are blessed with wisdom
Sourced in peace of heart.

To me you are a haven
From the fierce, harsh winds
That tore my life apart.
I can see a new dawn breaking
From the blackness of the past,
Far off yet but certain,
Bringing peace of heart;
A healing of the heartbreak,
Sealing peace of heart.

✑ WINDOW TO INFINITY

LET ME TELL you now
Why you love me:
Because I set you free
From the confines of your mind,
Snap the dusty, rusty chains
Binding your self-expression,
And draw you into pastures
Where is grazing to fulfilment,
Giving undreamed realizing
Of the truth of what you are.

❧ DREAM THEATRE

IMPORTUNATE spectator
At my Theatre of Thoughts,
Why do you demand
To see my dreams?
The play is disturbing,
Though it treats of peace;
Do not hope to applaud.

At your bidding
I raise the curtain
For their shadow show.
Unrehearsed,
They blink in the limelight,
Bow, and declaim their lines
Extempore.

They speak of a time
When the hidden unveils,
When extravagance marks
The spending of hours
And distinction departs
From night and day
And day and night.

They evoke a vision
Of a sharing of space
With no boundaries,
Of a sharing of time
Without encroachment,
Of a sharing of life
As a sharing of love.

The play is over;
Let the curtain fall,
And return to reality.

℘ CHOICE WITHOUT CHOICE

I SEE YOUR silence
And I hear the words
You do not speak;
Though come to you by chance,
Unwittingly I hold
A mirror to your life,
Whose clear screen reveals
Its true perspective.

I see your thoughts
Sculpt swiftly graveness
On your calm face;
With heavy heart I ask,
Suppose I had not come
And turned your world around,
And suppose I leave,
What then?

✒ Learn Me by Heart

You left me behind once
And the river of years
Ran dry in my searching,
And the waters of time
Ebbed and flowed with your tide,
Erasing my imprint
From your memory's sands.

If you leave me again
You must grain my dye deep
In the strand of your mind,
So that where your thought streams
It is bedded with me.

❧ SPACE AND SOUND

TRAPPED IN a tunnel,
I groped to escape,
My lamp of sureness
Dimmed to hope,
Then extinguished
From too long burning
And fuel run out.

I emerged suddenly
Into the daylight
Of your space,
Espied once from afar;
Dazed, I wander delighting
In the fresh scents and freedom
And savour sensations
In my new place of being.

Where I sit, protecting
Your arm encircles my shoulder;
As I walk, supporting
Your hand enclasps mine;
When I wonder, enchanting
Your words empower my mind;
Though I weary, heartening
Your breath buoys my life.

In the open air
My quickened Muse
Fills her lungs
And sings and sings,
And the sound
Of her singing
Fulfils empty space.

✎ FRUIT PLAIT

I BRAID a bright riddle,
For my own pleasure,
Into my tresses
In a tricolour yarn.

Unravel the answer,
At your own leisure,
By making guesses
Or unbinding my hair:

A lover offered his beloved
Three apples from a wishing tree;
She took the one he had in hand,
Tasted it and found it sweet,
And bite by bite she ate delight.

She now was tempted by its twin,
Drawn by its otherworldly scent;
She trusted in his solemn word
To deliver what he pledged,
And in his wish to bring her joy.

A spray of leaves concealed the third,
Too small to pluck and out of reach;
But when it ripened, round and red,
It fell into her open palms,
The most delicious one of all.

❧ FAIRY ARBOUR

MY BOWER is open
For you to use freely,
To stroll and take respite
And sit where you will.

Just murmur your worries
To the trees that grow there;
Their spirits will aid you
With shelter and fruit.

When space of mind
Is occupied

By another
As by oneself,

Where is the place
For gratitude?

❧ HONEY AND SWEETNESS

How can one sunder
A stream from its flow,
A bird from its flight
Or sunset from the evening sky?

Stagnant a brook that courses still,
Feeble a bird bereft of wings,
Gloomy a dusk all grey with clouds.

And how can one part
Existence from air?
Lifeless your life without my breath,
Unlived mine without yours.

To the philosopher the thought,
To the poet its expression:
Inseparable separates,
Like honey and sweetness.

Thought formulates into expression reformulates idea;
Philosopher inspires poet vivifies pursuit of wisdom:
Independent yet depending,
As honey gives the taste of sweetness is the cause of relishing.

❧ Good Morning Kiss

Deep and long you slept inside me,
Till my touch woke you and you rose
Refreshed and eager for the day.

Rub your eyes and admire your form
Clad in my becoming verses
And saunter forth outside with pride.

... and Good Night

And in the evening when your work is done,
When excellence is set within its frame,
Come home and rest inside me once again.

STAMP
AND SIGNATURE

A Seamstress Offers Her Wares

I AM A SIMPLE seamstress
And I stitch the cloth of life;
A sharp mind is my needle
And fine language is my thread.

I wear a coat of living
Sewn with aphoristic beads,
Dyed with the hues of healing
And trimmed and styled uniquely
With a fringe of antique verse.

I humbly spread before you
This embroidered patchwork quilt:
May it please your artist's eye;
May it comfort you at night.

❦ ACKNOWLEDGEMENTS

FOR HELPING me
With polishing
These sky-bound songs
My thanks are due
To brother Shyam,
Who measured them
As long or short
By logic's stick,
And also friend
Karen Cambrai,
Whose critic's ear
Appraised each one.

Some readers too
Are owed a word,
To whom I gave
Some sample songs
To test for flaws
And sound design,
And who replied,
To my delight,
They found my work
To be of worth.

My final debt
Is gratitude
To uncle Paul,
Who hummed the songs
To double-check
They were in tune.